A YEAR OF POSITIVE THINKING

365 quotes to live your life by

by

M. Ganendran

CONTENTS

Introduction

A good quote needs very little introduction. For many of us, our first meeting with a quote was in a book or a film; a collection of individual words that, on their own, would be ordinary, but when brought together in a special way, stay with you forever. Some people throughout the ages were blessed with an uncanny talent for observing life so clearly and expressing it so neatly that they created their own quotes, which have carried their name across the centuries and given them a little piece of immortality. As Benjamin Disraeli said, *"The wisdom of the wise, and the experience of ages, may be preserved by quotation."*

Whenever and wherever you originally discovered your love for quotes, this book is for you. If this is your first exploration into the world of quotes, it's for you too – and if so, I urge you to savour the experience you're about to have when new quotes "speak" to you for the very first time. There's a special sensation when you meet a quote that resonates with you, as if its author has somehow seen into your soul and hit on the very thing that makes sense to you at that moment. When you feel a little glimmer or sparkle in your mind and heart, you can be sure that what you're reading reflects your own truth. You don't have to agree with every quote, but with the help of your own inner wisdom, you'll just *know* when you read one that's meant for you.

Quotes can do many things for us. They can inspire us, motivate us, make us smile, gift us hope in trying times, and even challenge our perceptions, gently encouraging us to think about things a little differently.

I hope this collection of carefully chosen quotes does just that. But above all, I hope they remind you that we're all human. We may have myriad different lives, dreams, experiences, and troubles, but there is far more that we have in common than divides us.

Please enjoy this collection, whether you resolutely read only one quote for each day of the year, or whether you choose to ignore the dates and digest as many as you choose in one go. It's completely up to you!

The origin of each quote and the rights of the public to use it have been carefully checked. Any breach of copyright or errors in attribution are unintended and should be notified to the author.

Many of these quotes were written by people who lived in a different time from our own, and as such, their wording can seem outdated and not inclusive, for example in the use of "he", "him", "mankind" etc. Rather than misquoting them, I have left these as they are, with the understanding that this is an aspect of history that has since been improved. No offence is intended.

January

1 January

Don't let yesterday use up too much of today.

- Cherokee Indian Proverb

2 January

Thousands of candles can be lit from a single candle and the life of the candle will not be shortened. Happiness never decreases from being shared.

- Buddha

3 January

You're not going to master the rest of your life in one day. Master the day, then keep doing that every day.

- Unknown

4 January

To dare is to lose one's footing momentarily. To not dare is to lose oneself.

- Soren Kierkegaard

5 January

Don't just look for the blessing. Be the blessing.

- Unknown

6 January

The wound is the place where the light enters you.

- Rumi

7 January

Re-examine all you have been told.
Dismiss what insults your soul.

- Walt Whitman

8 January

It was only a sunny smile, and little it
cost in the giving, but like morning light
it scattered the night, and made the day
worth living.

- F. Scott Fitzgerald

9 January

The best time to plant a tree was twenty years ago. The next best time is now.

- Chinese proverb

10 January

The greatest good you can do for another is not just to share your riches but to reveal to him his own.

- Benjamin Disraeli

11 January

No matter how grouchy you're feeling,
you'll find the smile more or less healing.
It grows in a wreath all around the front
teeth - thus preserving the face from
congealing.

- Anthony Euwer

12 January

The world is full of magic things,
patiently waiting for our senses to grow
sharper.

- W.B. Yeats

13 January

Looking behind I am filled with gratitude. Looking forward I am filled with vision. Looking upwards I am filled with strength.

- Quero Apache prayer

14 January

Know your limits, but never stop trying to exceed them.

- Unknown

15 January

Start a huge, foolish project, like Noah…it makes absolutely no difference what people think of you.

- Rumi

16 January

The darker the night, the brighter the stars.

- Fyodor Dostoevsky

17 January

What you think, you become. What you feel, you attract. What you imagine, you create.

- Buddha

18 January

Just when the caterpillar thought the world was ending, it turned into a butterfly.

- Zhuang Zhou

19 January

I close my eyes in order to see.

- Paul Gauguin

20 January

I believe, and therefore anything is possible.

- Unknown

21 January

The most wasted of all days is one
without laughter.

- Nicolas Chamfort

22 January

In a rapidly ascending balloon were
two men. One watched the earth
getting further and further away.
One watched the stars getting nearer
and nearer.

- George Jean Nathan

23 January

Every new beginning comes from some other beginning's end.

– Seneca

24 January

Our doubts are traitors and make us lose the good we oft might win, by fearing to attempt.

- William Shakespeare, "Measure for Measure"

25 January

Don't lose hope. When the sun goes down, the stars come out.

- Unknown

26 January

I am not afraid of storms for I am learning how to sail my ship.

- Louisa May Alcott

27 January

Never be in a hurry. Do everything quietly and in a calm spirit. Do not lose your inner peace for anything whatsoever, even if your whole world seems upset.

- Saint Francis de Sales

28 January

You are more than who you were.

- Unknown

29 January

"Science, my lad, is made up of mistakes, but they are mistakes which it is useful to make, because they lead little by little to the truth."

- Journey to the Centre of the Earth, Jules Verne

30 January

Believe in your infinite potential. Your only limitations are those you set upon yourself.

– Buddha

31 January

"O" stands for Opportunity, which is absent in yesterday, available in tOday, and thrice in tOmOrrOw! Never lose hope.

- Unknown

February

1 February

Fools laugh at others. Wisdom laughs at itself.

– Osho

2 February

You aspire to great things? Begin with little ones.

- St. Augustine

3 February

The person who doesn't keep score, who's not looking to be richer, or afraid of losing, who has not the slightest interest even in his own personality: he's free.

– Rumi

4 February

There is no path to happiness; happiness is the path.

– Buddha

5 February

The sun shines and warms and lights us and we have no curiosity to know why this is so; but we ask the reason of all evil, of pain, and hunger, and mosquitoes and silly people.

- Ralph Waldo Emerson

6 February

Collect moments, not things.

- Unknown

7 February

What we see depends mainly on what we look for.

- John Lubbock

8 February

You are never too old to set another goal or to dream a new dream.

- C.S. Lewis

9 February

The chief danger in life is that you may take too many precautions.

- Alfred Adler

10 February

There are hundreds of paths up the mountain, all leading to the same place, so it doesn't matter which path you take. The only person wasting time is the one who runs around the mountain, telling everyone else that their path is wrong.

- Hindu proverb

11 February

Be patient and tough. Someday this pain
will be useful to you.

- Ovid

12 February

Appreciate where you are in your
journey, even if it's not where you want
to be. Every season serves a purpose.

- Unknown

13 February

Holding on to anger is like grasping a hot coal with the intent of throwing it at someone else; you are the one who gets burned.

- Buddha

14 February

May the holes in your net be no larger than the fish in it.

– Irish blessing

15 February

Simplicity is making the journey of this life with just baggage enough.

– Charles Dudley Warner

16 February

Be humble, for you are made of dung. Be noble, for you are made of stars.

- Serbian Saying

17 February

However many holy words you read,
however many you speak, what good
will they do if you do not act upon them?

– Buddha

18 February

A small body of determined spirits fired
by an unquenchable faith in their mission
can alter the course of history.

- Mahatma Gandhi

19 February

The privilege of a lifetime is to become
who you really are.

- Carl Jung

20 February

I am not an Athenian or a Greek, I am a
citizen of the world.

- Socrates

21 February

Tomorrow is fresh, with no mistakes in it.

- L.M. Montgomery

22 February

There is only one success - to be able to spend your life in your own way.

- Christopher Morley

23 February

Wherever a man turns, he can find someone who needs him.

- Albert Schweitzer

24 February

He who gives when he is asked has waited too long.

– Seneca

25 February

Let me be thankful first, because I never was robbed before; second, because although they took my purse, they did not take my life; third, although they took my all, it was not much; and fourthly, it was I who was robbed, not I who robbed.

- Matthew Henry

26 February

Those who wish to sing always find a song.

- Swedish proverb

27 February

When you get into a tight place and everything goes against you, 'til it seems as though you could not hang on a minute longer, never give up, for that is just the place and time the tide will turn.

- Harriet Beecher Stowe

28 February

Before you speak, let your words pass through three gates: "Is it true?" "Is it necessary?" "Is it kind?"

- Rumi

March

1 March

Every single thing changes and is changing always in this world. Yet with the same light the moon goes on shining.

- Saigyo

2 March

By being yourself, you put something wonderful in the world that was not there before.

- Edwin Elliott

3 March

The saints were not abnormal beings, cases to be studied. They were, they are - normal - of flesh, like yours. And they won.

- St. Josemaria Escriva

4 March

A single event can awaken within us a stranger totally unknown to us. To live is to be slowly born.

- Antoine de Saint-Exupéry

5 March

Nothing is, unless our thinking
makes it so.

- William Shakespeare

6 March

To find the universal elements enough; to
find the air and the water exhilarating; to
be refreshed by a morning walk or an
evening saunter... to be thrilled by the
stars at night; to be elated over a bird's
nest or a wildflower in spring - these are
some of the rewards of the simple life.

- John Burroughs

7 March

I am but one, but I am one. I cannot do
everything, but I can do something. What
I can do I ought to do, and what I ought
to do, God help me, I will do.

- Edward Everett Hale

8 March

Raise your words, not your voice. It is
rain that grows flowers, not thunder.

- Rumi

9 March

The part you play, however small, is
greater far than none at all.

- A Poet's Proverbs, 1924

10 March

Be not afraid of anything. You will do
marvelous work.

- Swami Vivekananda

11 March

Don't carry your mistakes around with you. Instead, lay them on the ground and use them as stepping stones so you can rise above them.

- Unknown

12 March

If the world seems cold to you, kindle fires to warm it.

- Lucy Larcom

13 March

You are not created for everyone to like
you. Just be yourself and the right ones
will.

- Unknown

14 March

It is not the man who has little, but he
who desires more, that is poor.

- Seneca

15 March

Continuity gives us roots; change gives us branches, letting us stretch and grow and reach new heights.

- Pauline R. Kezer

16 March

Nothing is so often irretrievably missed as a daily opportunity.

- Marie von Ebner-Eschenbach

17 March

The present is the laboratory of the future.

- James Lendall Basford

18 March

May your blessings outnumber the shamrocks that grow and may trouble avoid you wherever you go.

– Irish blessing

19 March

You are searching the world for treasures, but the real treasure is Yourself.

- Rumi

20 March

Life is a shipwreck, but we must not forget to sing in the lifeboats.

- Voltaire

21 March

A wise man will make more
opportunities than he finds.

- Sir Francis Bacon

22 March

An arrow can only be shot by pulling it
backward. So when life is dragging you
back with difficulties, it means that it's
going to launch you into something great.

- Unknown

23 March

Be what you are. This is the first step toward becoming better than you are.

- Julius Charles Hare

24 March

To become learned, each day add something. To become enlightened, each day drop something.

- Lao Tzu

25 March

Everyone is a unique being, only once on this earth. By no extraordinary chance will such a marvelously picturesque piece of diversity in unity as they are, ever be put together a second time.

- Friedrich Nietzsche

26 March

The man who has done his level best, and who is conscious that he has done his best, is a success, even though the world may write him down as a failure.

- B.C. Forbes

27 March

Fear makes the wolf bigger than he is.

- German Proverb

28 March

If you don't go outside in the cold and rain once in a while, you'll never appreciate the pleasure of going back into the warmth.

- Unknown

29 March

The world is a book and those who do not travel read only one page.

- Saint Augustine

30 March

Nobody is superior, nobody is inferior. But nobody is equal either. People are simply unique, incomparable. You are You, I am I.

– Osho

31 March

There is peace even in the storm.

- Vincent Van Gogh

April

1 April

The bamboo that bends is stronger than
the oak that resists.

- Japanese Proverb

2 April

Remember this, that very little is needed
to make a happy life.

- Marcus Aurelius

3 April

Sorrow pulls up the rotten roots, so that new roots hidden beneath have room to grow. Whatever sorrow shakes from your heart, far better things will take their place.

– Rumi

4 April

Say little and do much. Receive all people with a cheerful countenance.

– Shammai

5 April

Do not condemn the judgment of another because it differs from your own. You may both be wrong.

- Dandemis

6 April

If today all you did was hold yourself together, be proud of yourself

- Unknown

7 April

Adopt the pace of nature: her secret
is patience.

- Ralph Waldo Emerson

8 April

Why should I be weary when every cell
of my body is bursting with life?

– Rumi

9 April

Never bend your head. Always hold it high. Look the world straight in the eye.

- Helen Keller

10 April

When there is no enemy within, the enemies outside cannot hurt you.

- African Proverb

11 April

If the doors of perception were cleansed,
everything would appear as it truly
is...infinite.

- William Blake

12 April

He who fears he will suffer, already
suffers because he fears.

- Michel de Montaigne

13 April

Peace comes from within. Do not seek it without.

- Buddha

14 April

In the hopes of reaching the moon, we fail to see the flowers that blossom at our feet.

- Albert Schweitzer

15 April

What is life? It is the flash of a firefly in the night. It is the breath of a buffalo in the wintertime. It is the little shadow which runs across the grass and loses itself in the sunset

- Blackfoot

16 April

Some people look for a beautiful place. Others make a place beautiful

- Hazrat Inayat Khan

17 April

My first blessing of the day: I woke up.

- Unknown

18 April

We generate fears while we sit. We overcome them by action.

- Dr Henry Link

19 April

Very little grows on jagged rock. Be
ground. Be crumbled, so wildflowers will
come up where you are.

- Rumi

20 April

If you try, you risk failure. If you don't,
you ensure it.

- Unknown

21 April

You cannot prevent the birds of sorrow from flying over your head, but you can prevent them from building nests in your hair.

- Chinese proverb

22 April

A wise man will be master of his mind. A fool will be its slave.

- Pubilius Syrus

23 April

The best view comes after the hardest climb.

- Unknown

24 April

Even if all the doors are closed, a secret path will be there for you that no one knows. You can't see it yet, but so many paradises are at the end of this path.

- Rumi

25 April

Dig the well before you are thirsty.

- Chinese proverb

26 April

Many eyes go through the meadow, but few see the flowers in it.

- Ralph Waldo Emerson

27 April

Don't just wish for a great day. Make it so.

- Unknown

28 April

Traveller, there are no paths. Paths are made by walking.

- Aboriginal proverb

29 April

When you feel a peaceful joy, that's when you are near truth.

.

- Rumi

30 April

All things are difficult before they are easy.

- Thomas Fuller

May

1 May

Act as if what you do makes a difference. It does.

- William James

2 May

There is nothing impossible to they who will try.

- Alexander the Great

3 May

You have power over your mind - not outside events. Realise this, and you will find strength.

- Marcus Aurelius

4 May

Do not worry if all the candles in the world flicker and die. We have the spark that starts the fire.

- Rumi

5 May

In order for the light to shine so brightly,
the darkness must be present.

- Francis Bacon

6 May

May you have the courage this week to
begin breaking patterns in your life that
no longer serve you. Give yourself
permission to pause and reflect today.

- Unknown

7 May

Be grateful! It is easy to thank after obtaining what you want, thank before having what you want.

- Rumi

8 May

The function of man is to live, not to exist. I shall not waste my days trying to prolong them. I shall use my time.

- Jack London

9 May

The best and most beautiful things in the world cannot be seen or even touched – they must be felt with the heart.

- Helen Keller

10 May

If a man could have half his wishes, he would double his troubles.

- Benjamin Franklin

11 May

Everything on the earth has a purpose, every disease a herb to cure it, and every person a mission. This is the Indian theory of existence.

- Mourning Dove Salish

12 May

The spirit is so near that you can't see it! But reach for it - don't be a jar full of water whose rim is always dry. Don't be the rider who gallops all night and never sees the horse that is beneath him.

- Rumi

13 May

Nature gives to every time and season
some beauties of its own.

- Charles Dickens

14 May

With freedom, books, flowers, and the
moon, who could not be happy?

- Oscar Wilde

15 May

Before enlightenment — chop wood, carry water. After enlightenment — chop wood, carry water.

- Zen Buddhist Proverb

16 May

There is no "right time", there is just time and what you choose to do with it.

- Benjamin Franklin

17 May

Never think that what you have to offer is insignificant. There will always be someone out there who needs what you have to give.

- Unknown

18 May

I will not carry a thing to its culmination simply because I entered in. I may have said I wanted it, but I will have the courage to say, "I've changed my mind."

- Muriel Strode

19 May

Wear gratitude like a cloak and it will
feed every corner of your life.

- *Rumi*

20 May

People of accomplishment rarely sit back
and let things happen to them. They go
out and happen to things.

- *Leonardo da Vinci*

21 May

You're not going to master the rest of your life in one day. Relax. Master the day, then keep doing that every day.

- Unknown

22 May

Normality is a paved road: it's comfortable to walk but no flowers grow.

- Vincent van Gogh

23 May

When you arise in the morning, give thanks for the food and for the joy of living. If you see no reason for giving thanks, the fault lies only in yourself.

- Chief Tecumseh

24 May

I am a part of all that I have met.

- Alfred Lord Tennyson

25 May

All life is an experiment. The more experiments you make the better. What if you get your coat soiled or torn? What if you do fail, and get rolled in the dirt once or twice? Up again, you shall never be so afraid of a tumble.

- Ralph Waldo Emerson

26 May

By three things the wise person may be known. He sees a shortcoming as it is. When he sees it, he tries to correct it. And when another acknowledges a shortcoming, the wise one forgives it as he should.

- Buddha

27 May

It is far better to give work that is above a person, than to educate the person to be above their work.

- John Ruskin

28 May

On a day when the wind is perfect, the sail just needs to open and the world is full of beauty. Today is such a day.

- Rumi

29 May

You can never cross the ocean until you have the courage to lose sight of the shore.

- Christopher Columbus

30 May

Silently, one by one, in the infinite meadows of heaven, blossomed the lovely stars, the forget-me-nots of the angels.

- Henry Wadsworth Longfellow

31 May

Be grateful for your life, every detail of it,
and your face will come to shine like a
sun, and everyone who sees it will be
made glad and peaceful.

- Rumi

June

1 June

We are just visitors to this time, this place. We are just passing through. Our purpose here is to observe, to learn, to grow...and then we return home.

- Australian Aboriginal proverb

2 June

To believe with certainty, we must begin with doubting.

- Stanislaw Leszczynski

3 June

My barn having burned down, I can now
see the moon.

- Mizuta Masahide

4 June

That man is the richest whose pleasures
are the cheapest.

– Henry David Thoreau

5 June

Keep your eyes on the stars and your feet on the ground.

- Theodore Roosevelt

6 June

Be like a tree and let the dead leaves drop.

- Rumi

7 June

The one who reads a lot and walks a lot,
sees a lot and knows a lot.

- Spanish proverb

8 June

It is our attitude at the beginning of a
difficult task which, more than anything
else, will affect its successful outcome.

- William James

9 June

It's no use going back to yesterday,
because I was a different person then.

- *Lewis Carroll*

10 June

Great things are done by a series of small
things brought together.

- *Vincent Van Gogh*

11 June

Very often, a change of self is needed
more than a change of scene.

- Arthur Christopher Benson

12 June

In a gentle way, you can shake the world.

- Mahatma Gandhi

13 June

How far that little candle throws his beams! So shines a good deed in a weary world.

- William Shakespeare, Merchant of Venice

14 June

Every truth has two sides; it is as well to look at both, before we commit ourselves to either.

- Aesop

15 June

It is only with the heart that one can see rightly; what is essential is invisible to the eye.

– Antoine de Saint-Exupéry, "The Little Prince"

16 June

The mark of a successful man is one that has spent an entire day on the bank of a river without feeling guilty about it.

- Unknown

17 June

All religions, all this singing, one song.
The differences are just illusion and
vanity. The sun's light looks a little
different on this wall than it does on that
wall, and a lot different on this other one,
but it's still one light.

- Rumi

18 June

Art is art, even when unsuccessful.

- Danish Proverb

19 June

No one should be ashamed to admit they are wrong, which is but saying, in other words, that they are wiser today than they were yesterday.

- Alexander Pope

20 June

For every minute you remain angry, you give up sixty seconds of peace of mind.

- Ralph Waldo Emerson

21 June

One life is all we have, and we live it as we believe in living it. But to sacrifice what you are and to live without belief, that is a fate more terrible than dying.

- Joan of Arc

22 June

"What makes the desert beautiful," said the little prince, "is that somewhere it hides a well…"

- Antoine de Saint-Exupéry, The Little Prince

23 June

A good laugh is sunshine in the house.

- William Makepeace Thackeray

24 June

The best way to cheer yourself up is to try to cheer somebody else up.

- Mark Twain

25 June

All that was great in the past was ridiculed, condemned, combated, suppressed – only to emerge all the more powerfully, all the more triumphantly from the struggle.

- Nikola Tesla

26 June

I am defeated, and know it, if I meet any human being from whom I find myself unable to learn anything.

- George Herbert Palmer

27 June

Even when tied in a thousand knots, the string is still but one.

- Rumi

28 June

When the winds of change blow, some people build walls and others build windmills.

- Chinese Proverb

29 June

HAPPINESS—A butterfly, which when pursued, seems always just beyond your grasp; but if you sit down quietly, may alight upon you.

- A Chapter of Definitions, Daily Crescent, 1848

30 June

All through history, truth and love have always won. There have been tyrants and murderers and for a time, they seem invincible, but in the end, they always fall.

- Mahatma Gandhi

July

1 July

We must remain as close to the flowers, the grass, and the butterflies as the child who is not much taller than they. We adults have outgrown them and must stoop down to them. Whoever would partake of all good things must understand how to be small at times.

- Friedrich Nietzsche

2 July

He who does not know one thing knows another.

- African proverb

3 July

It is during our darkest moments that we must focus to see the light.

- Aristotle

4 July

I will not let anyone walk through my mind with their dirty feet.

- Mahatma Gandhi

5 July

If a man doesn't keep pace with his companions, perhaps it's because he hears a different drummer. Let him step to the music which he hears, however measured or far away.

- Henry David Thoreau

6 July

How foolish is man! He ruins the present while worrying about the future, but weeps in the future by recalling his past!

- Ali Ibn Abi Talib

7 July

For many people, the acquisition of wealth does not end their troubles, it only changes them.

- Seneca

8 July

There's no need to fear the wind if your haystacks are tied down.

- Irish proverb

9 July

From a small seed, a mighty trunk may grow.

- Aeschylus

10 July

Kindness is a language which the deaf can hear and the blind can see.

- Mark Twain

11 July

I am still learning.

- Michelangelo, at age 87

12 July

A man who dares to waste one hour of
time has not discovered the value of life.

- Charles Darwin

13 July

Everyone takes the limits of their own field of vision for the limits of the world.

- Arthur Schopenhauer

14 July

The human being is a guest-house; each day new arrivals. Joy, depression, a moment of awareness come as unexpected visitors. Welcome them! Even if sorrows sweep your house empty of its furniture, treat them honorably. They may be clearing you out for new delights.

- Rumi

15 July

Flowers often grow more beautifully on dung-hills than in gardens that look beautifully kept.

- Saint Francis de Sales

16 July

It is not enough for a man to know how to ride; he must know how to fall.

- Mexican Proverb

17 July

Look at the sparrows; they do not know
what they will do in the next moment.
Let us literally live from moment to
moment.

- Mahatma Gandhi

18 July

Every misfortune is a blessing.

- African proverb

19 July

The aim of an argument or discussion should not be victory, but progress.

- Joseph Joubert

20 July

Every noble work is at first impossible.

- Thomas Carlyle

21 July

Each day provides its own gifts.

- Marcus Aurelius

22 July

Every heart that has beat strongly and cheerfully has left a hopeful impulse behind it in the world and bettered the tradition of humankind.

- Robert Louis Stevenson

23 July

The fool doth think he is wise, but the wise man knows himself to be a fool.

- William Shakespeare, "As You Like It"

24 July

He that in his studies wholly applies himself to labor and exercise, and neglects meditation, loses his time; and he that only applies himself to meditation, and neglects labor and exercise, only wanders and loses himself.

- Confucius

25 July

Big ideas have small beginnings.

- Unknown

26 July

If you fell down yesterday, stand up today.

– H. G. Wells

27 July

To begin, begin.

- *William Wordsworth*

28 July

It's no use carrying an umbrella if your shoes are leaking.

— Irish proverb

29 July

Of all the liars in the world, sometimes the worst are our own fears.

- *Rudyard Kipling*

30 July

Experience is the hardest kind of teacher. It gives you the test first and the lesson afterwards.

- *Oscar Wilde*

31 July

The distance is nothing; it is only the first
step that is difficult.

- Marquise du Deffand

August

1 August

If you have built castles in the air, your work need not be lost; that is where they should be. Now put the foundations under them.

- Henry David Thoreau

2 August

There is a loftier ambition than merely to stand high in the world. It is to stoop down and lift mankind a little higher.

- Henry Van Dyke

3 August

Do not wait to strike until the iron is hot; make it hot by striking.

- W.B. Yeats

4 August

Kindred spirits are not so scarce as I used to think. It's splendid to find out there are so many of them in the world.

- L.M. Montgomery, "Anne of Green Gables"

5 August

Let what is past flow away downstream.

- Japanese proverb

6 August

Perseverance is a great element of success. If you only knock long enough and loud enough at the gate, you are sure to wake up somebody.

- Henry Wadsworth Longfellow

7 August

If everyone gives one thread, the poor man will have a shirt.

- Russian proverb

8 August

A lake forms drop by drop.

- Turkish proverb

9 August

Those who do not move, do not notice their chains.

- *Rosa Luxemburg*

10 August

Water is the softest thing, yet it can penetrate mountains and earth. This shows clearly the principle of softness overcoming hardness.

- *Lao Tzu*

11 August

When I think of the others' misfortunes, I forget mine.

- African proverb

12 August

If you want something you've never had, then you've got to do something you've never done.

- Thomas Jefferson

13 August

A seed hidden in the heart of an apple is an orchard invisible.

- Welsh proverb

14 August

Life without endeavour is like entering a jewel mine and coming out with empty hands.

- Japanese proverb

15 August

He who knows all the answers has not been asked all the questions.

- Confucius

?

16 August

If every man would sweep his own doorstep the city would soon be clean.

- Welsh proverb

17 August

He is great who speaks great, greater who thinks great, and greatest who lives great.

- James Lendall Basford

18 August

We are all inventors sailing out on a voyage of discovery, each guided by a private chart, of which there is no duplicate. The world is all gates, all opportunities.

- Ralph Waldo Emerson

19 August

There is hope as long as your fishing-line
is in the water.

- Norwegian proverb

20 August

Even the darkest night will end, and the
sun will rise.

- Victor Hugo

21 August

There are four questions of value in life…
What is sacred? Of what is the spirit
made? What is worth living for, and what
is worth dying for? The answer to each is
the same. Only love.

- Lord Byron

22 August

He who thinks too much about every step
he takes will always stay on one leg.

- Chinese proverb

23 August

Never say, "Oops," always say, "Ah, interesting!"

- Unknown

24 August

It is only when the mind and character slumber that the dress can be seen.

- Ralph Waldo Emerson

25 August

Conquer the angry one by not getting angry; conquer the wicked by goodness; conquer the stingy by generosity, and the liar by speaking the truth.

- Buddha

26 August

Next time you think of wonderful things, don't forget to think of yourself.

- Unknown

27 August

Always eat the best grape first; this way there'll be none better left on the bunch, and each grape seems good down to the last. If you eat the other way, you won't have a good grape in the lot.

- Samuel Butler

28 August

Never let the future disturb you. You will meet it, if you have to, with the same weapons of reason which today arm you against the present.

– Marcus Aurelius Antoninus

29 August

I have no dress except the one I wear every day. If you are going to be kind enough to give me one, please let it be practical and dark so that I can put it on afterwards to go to the laboratory.

- Marie Curie

30 August

A boat cannot go forward if each rows his own way.

- African proverb

31 August

If there was nothing wrong in the world there wouldn't be anything for us to do.

- George Bernard Shaw

september

1 September

We meet no ordinary people in our lives.

- C.S. Lewis

2 September

You are not only responsible for what you say, but also for what you do not say.

- Martin Luther

3 September

Starting the work is two-thirds of it.

– Welsh proverb

4 September

We do not quit playing because we grow old, we grow old because we quit playing.

- Oliver Wendell Holmes, Sr

5 September

The best way out is always through.

- Robert Frost

6 September

The man who counts the bits of food he swallows is never satisfied.

- African proverb

7 September

If your sword's too short, add to its length by taking one step forward.

- Unknown

8 September

May the blessing of light be on you, light without and light within.

— Irish Blessing

9 September

Simplicity and harmony are the ultimate conditions to be attained in all things.

- Horace Fletcher

10 September

Bloom where you are planted.

- Saint Francis de Sales

11 September

We have two ears and one mouth so that we can listen twice as much as we speak.

- Epictetus

12 September

Well done is better than well said.

- Benjamin Franklin

13 September

Do not sacrifice the entire rose to find
fault with the thorn.

- Unknown

14 September

The butterfly counts not months but
moments and has time enough.

- Rabindranath Tagore

15 September

Dare to be honest and fear no labour.

- Robert Burns

16 September

Your worst enemy cannot harm you as much as your own unguarded thoughts.

- Buddha

17 September

The earth is the mother of all people, and all people should have equal rights upon it.

- Chief Joseph

18 September

No matter how long the winter, spring is sure to follow.

- Proverb (unknown origin)

19 September

An adventure is only an inconvenience rightly considered. An inconvenience is only an adventure wrongly considered.

- G.K. Chesterton

20 September

Turn your face to the sun and the shadows fall behind you.

- Maori proverb

21 September

The best way to gain self-confidence is to do what you are afraid to do.

- Unknown

22 September

If you cry because the sun has gone out of your life, your tears will prevent you from seeing the stars.

- Rabindranath Tagore

23 September

Worry often gives a small thing a big shadow.

- Swedish Proverb

24 September

A true warrior, like tea, shows his strength in hot water.

- Chinese Proverb

25 September

The three great essentials to achieve anything worthwhile are hard work, "stick-to-itiveness" and common sense.

- Thomas Edison

26 September

To know what you prefer, instead of humbly saying 'Amen' to what the world tells you that you ought to prefer, is to keep your soul alive.

- Robert Louis Stevenson

27 September

Sticks in a bundle are unbreakable.

- Kenyan proverb

28 September

To do nothing is sometimes a good remedy.

- Hippocrates

29 September

Am I not destroying my enemies when I make friends of them?

- Abraham Lincoln

30 September

Be still like a mountain and flow like a great river.

- Lao Tzu

October

1 October

Ideals are like stars; you won't succeed in touching them with your hands. But like the seafaring man on the desert of waters, you choose them as your guides, and following them you'll reach your destiny.

- Carl Schurz

2 October

I prayed for twenty years but received no answer until I prayed with my legs.

- Frederick Douglass

3 October

Problems are only opportunities with thorns on them.

– Hugh Miller

4 October

Remember the tea kettle; although it is up to its neck in hot water it keeps on singing.

- Unknown

5 October

A man would do nothing if he waited until he could do it so well that no one could find fault.

- John Henry Newman

6 October

Life is really simple, but we insist on making it complicated.

- Confucius

7 October

Life is not long, and too much of it must not pass in idle deliberation how it shall be spent.

- Samuel Johnson

8 October

Colours are the smiles of nature.

- Leigh Hunt

9 October

Don't find fault. Find a remedy.

- Henry Ford

10 October

Life begets life. Energy creates energy. It is by spending oneself that one becomes rich.

- Sarah Bernhardt

11 October

To conquer oneself is a greater task than conquering others.

- Buddha

12 October

Half the failures in life arise from pulling in the horse as it is leaping.

- Augustus William Hare and Julies Charles Hare

13 October

Do not regret growing older. It is a
privilege denied to many.

- Unknown

14 October

Fear less, hope more; eat less, chew more;
whine less, breathe more; talk less, say
more; hate less, love more; and all good
things are yours.

- Swedish Proverb

15 October

Take time to eat, and to rest and play.
Take time for politeness. Take time to
pass over the road of life - and if you fall,
arise again and struggle on; let not hurry
nor worry divert you from your path.

- Health Magazine, 1899

16 October

If I can't make it through one door, I'll go
through another – or I'll make a door.
Something terrific will come no matter
how dark the present.

- Rabindranath Tagore

17 October

The winds of grace are always blowing,
but you have to raise the sail.

- Ramakrishna

18 October

Nature gave men two ends - one to sit on
and one to think with. Ever since then
man's success or failure has been
dependent on the one he used most.

- George R. Kirkpatrick

19 October

The best of healers is good cheer.

- Pindar

20 October

Sometimes even to live is an act of courage.

- Seneca

21 October

Finish each day before you begin the next and interpose a solid wall of sleep between the two.

- Ralph Waldo Emerson

22 October

Though outwardly a gloomy shroud, the inner half of every cloud is bright and shining: I therefore turn my clouds about and always wear them inside out to show the lining.

- Ellen Thorneycroft Fowler

23 October

I saw the angel in the marble and carved until I set him free.

- Michelangelo

24 October

Tragedy is like strong acid – it dissolves away all but the very gold of truth.

- D.H. Lawrence

25 October

I ask not for a lighter burden, but for broader shoulders.

- Jewish Proverb

26 October

Nothing is more difficult, and therefore more precious, than to be able to decide.

- Napoleon Bonaparte

27 October

There are those who are so scrupulously afraid of doing wrong that they seldom venture to do anything.

- Luc de Clapiers

28 October

We turn not older with years, but newer every day.

- Emily Dickinson

29 October

I wish I had lingered a week or so…but we mortals are always in haste to reach somewhere else, forgetting that the zest is in the journey, not in the destination.

- Ralph D. Paine, Roads of Adventure

30 October

Trees are happy for no reason; they're not going to become presidents and they're not going to become rich. Look at the flowers. It is simply unbelievable how happy flowers are.

- Osho

31 October

Sometimes I go about pitying myself, and all the while I am being carried across the sky by beautiful clouds.

- Ojibwe saying

November

1 November

Your mind is a garden, your thoughts are the seeds, the harvest can be either flowers or weeds.

- William Wordsworth

2 November

Most people pursue enjoyment with such breathless haste that they hurry past it.

- Soren Kierkegaard

3 November

Real difficulties can be overcome, it is only the imaginary ones that are unconquerable.

- Theodore Newton Vail

4 November

It is impossible for anyone to begin to learn what he thinks he already knows.

- Epictetus

5 November

May you have warm words on a cool evening, a full moon on a dark night, and a smooth road all the way to your door.

- Irish Toast

6 November

Anyone who stops learning is old, whether at 20 or at 80. Anyone who keeps on learning not only remains young, but becomes constantly more valuable, regardless of physical capacity.

- Henry Ford

7 November

If there is no struggle, there is no progress.

- Frederick Douglass

8 November

Whatever you are, try to be a good one.

- William Makepeace Thackeray

9 November

Don't judge each day by the harvest you reap but by the seeds that you plant.

- Robert Louis Stevenson

10 November

Have regular hours for work and play; make each day both useful and pleasant, and prove you understand the worth of time by using it well. Then youth will be delightful, old age will bring few regrets, and life will become a beautiful success.

- Louisa May Alcott

11 November

Earth and sky, woods and fields, lakes and rivers, the mountain and the sea are excellent schoolmasters, and teach us more than we can ever learn from books.

- John Lubbock

12 November

Forget not that the earth delights to feel your bare feet and the winds long to play with your hair.

- Khalil Gibran

13 November

Work on yourself first, take responsibility for your own progress.

- I Ching

14 November

But what minutes! Count them by sensation, and not by calendars, and each moment is a day.

- Benjamin Disraeli

177

15 November

If we all did the things we are capable of doing, we would literally astound ourselves.

- *Thomas Edison*

16 November

The true harvest of my daily life is as intangible and indescribable as the tints of morning or evening. It is a little stardust caught, a segment of the rainbow which I have clutched.

- *Henry David Thoreau*

17 November

Nothing is a waste of time if you use the experience wisely.

- Auguste Rodin

18 November

I will permit no man to narrow and degrade my soul by making me hate him.

- Booker T. Washington

19 November

Nature does not hurry, yet everything is accomplished.

- Lao Tzu

20 November

If the wind will not serve, take to the oars.

- Latin Proverb

21 November

Have nothing in your house that you do not know to be useful or believe to be beautiful.

- William Morris

22 November

Poor and content is rich, and rich enough.

- William Shakespeare

23 November

May your thoughts be as glad as the
shamrocks, may your heart be as light as
a song, may each day bring you bright
happy hours that stay with you all the
year long.

- Irish Blessing

24 November

There is no such thing in anyone's life as
an unimportant day.

- Alexander Woollcott

25 November

The best things in life are nearest: light in your eyes, flowers at your feet, duties at your hand. Don't grasp at the stars, do life's plain, common work - daily duties and daily bread are the sweetest things.

- Robert Louis Stevenson

26 November

Age is opportunity no less than youth itself, though in another dress. And as the evening twilight fades away, the sky is filled with stars, invisible by day.

- Henry Wadsworth Longfellow

27 November

Don't look where you fell, but where you slipped.

- African Proverb

28 November

Finish each day and be done with it. You did what you could; some blunders no doubt crept in; forget them as soon as you can. Tomorrow is a new day; begin it serenely, with too high a spirit to be encumbered with your old nonsense.

- Ralph Waldo Emerson

29 November

The drops of rain make a hole in the
stone not by violence but by oft falling.

- Lucretius

30 November

When you reach the end of your rope, tie
a knot in it and hang on.

- Franklin D. Roosevelt

December

1 December

We are what we repeatedly do.
Excellence then, is not an act, but a habit.

- Aristotle

2 December

I am not what happened to me, I am who
I choose to become.

- Carl Jung

3 December

Although the world is full of suffering, it is also full of the overcoming of it.

- Helen Keller

4 December

Light tomorrow with today.

- Elizabeth Barrett Browning

5 December

Better a diamond with a flaw than a
pebble without.

- Confucius

6 December

The shell must break before the bird can
fly.

- Alfred Tennyson

7 December

How glorious a greeting the sun gives the mountains!

- John Muir

8 December

Dare to be what you are and learn to resign with a good grace all that you are not.

- Henri-Frédéric Amiel

9 December

There is no saint without a past, and no sinner without a future.

- *Oscar Wilde*

10 December

Don't miss the doughnut by looking through the hole.

- *Unknown*

11 December

When through one man a little more
goodness, a little more light and truth
comes into the world, then that man's life
has had meaning.

- Alfred Delp

12 December

The greatest mistake you can make in life
is to be continually fearing you will make
one.

- Elbert Hubbard

13 December

Put a grain of boldness into everything you do.

- Baltasar Gracian

14 December

I have never in my life learned anything from anyone who agreed with me.

- Dudley Field Malone

15 December

Age is an issue of mind over matter.
If you don't mind, it doesn't matter.

- Mark Twain

16 December

I keep the telephone of my mind open to
peace, harmony, health and abundance.
Then, whenever doubt, anxiety or fear try
to call me, they keep getting a busy signal
- and soon they'll forget my number.

- Edith Armstrong Talbot

17 December

The man who removes a mountain
begins by carrying away small stones.

- Chinese Proverb

18 December

Why should I stay at the bottom of a well
when a strong rope is in my hand?

- Rumi

19 December

May you always have work for your hands to do, may your pockets hold always a coin or two. May the sun shine bright on your windowpane, may the rainbow be certain to follow each rain.

- Irish Blessing

20 December

When eating bamboo sprouts, remember the person who planted them.

- Chinese Proverb

21 December

Some people see things as they are and say "why"; I dream things that never were and say "why not?"

- George Bernard Shaw

22 December

I am always doing that which I cannot do, in order that I may learn how to do it.

- Pablo Picasso

23 December

A smooth sea never made a skilful sailor.

- Franklin D. Roosevelt

24 December

The hardest prisons to break out of are
the ones we build ourselves.

- Unknown

25 December

I never had a policy; I have just tried to do my very best each and every day.

- Abraham Lincoln

26 December

Let your boat of life be light, packed with only what you need - a homely home and simple pleasures, enough to eat and enough to wear. You'll find the boat easier to pull and have time to think as well as to work.

- Jerome K. Jerome, "Three Men in a Boat"

27 December

Nothing is really work unless you would rather be doing something else.

- J.M. Barrie

28 December

Courage is fear holding on a minute longer.

- General George Smith Patton

29 December

The question for each of us is not what we would do if we had the means, time, and educational advantages, but what we will do with the things we have.

- Hamilton Wright Mabie

30 December

I have no right, by anything I do or say, to demean a human being in their own eyes. What matters is not what I think of them it is what they think of themselves.

- Antoine de Saint-Exupéry

31 December

Hope smiles from the threshold of
the year to come, whispering, "It
will be happier."

- Alfred Tennyson

About the Author

M. Ganendran began writing as a child and hasn't stopped since, except for tea breaks, naturally. She has been shortlisted for several short story and flash fiction competitions and now writes mystery and adventure novels for children and young adults, often with a hint of the historical and supernatural.

She also works with her husband, writer and researcher Prash Ganendran, on his true crime books and they have co-authored a Victorian murder mystery, "The Porcelain Cat", and a book of fiendish lateral thinking puzzles, "No Albatrosses Allowed."

In her spare time, she enjoys walks in nature, birdwatching, cooking, mindfulness, meditation and reiki – and of course, she loves a good quote.

Can I Ask A Favour?

If you enjoyed this book, I would really appreciate it if you could rate and review it on Amazon. As an independent author, it means a lot to receive feedback from readers.

Thanks for your support!

Want to try some exciting (yet gentle) fiction from this author?

The Porcelain Cat: A Detective Amarnath Mystery

As October of 1900 draws to a close, London's foggy, lamplit streets are hit by a string of burglaries which puzzle Scotland Yard. When they culminate in a gruesome murder, Sherlock Holmes is called in to investigate. But has he put the wrong man behind bars? In this atmospheric mystery, an Indian Detective seeks answers with the help of his assistant Madeleine Carmichael. With a touch of humour and a great deal of determination, the unconventional duo must use the most modern techniques to unravel the depths of human cunning.

Praise for the book:
"Very much enjoyed this husband and wife creation. I would love to see this (and subsequent stories) as BBC productions. The writing put me right into the characters' world and was wonderfully and strikingly visual."

The Song of the Mermaid

When Stef Brightbay goes to visit her Aunt May in the village of Zennor in Cornwall, she expects to have an uneventful trip. But when her mother persuades her to research their family history and she begins to uncover a tragic event that took place there in 1812, she is determined to find out more. She also learns of the local folklore; the legend of Matthew Trewhella who was enticed to his death by a beautiful mermaid.

Why is her aunt so uncommunicative? What secret is being hidden by a strange local family who seem to want to put a stop to her investigation? And even more mysteriously, why are unusual things happening at her aunt's cottage? With the help of sea-salt fisherman Arthur and his faithful chocolate Labrador, Stef pieces together the past and realises that a frightening parallel is unravelling in the present day. Will they be able to take action before it's too late?

A Summer of Witches

Wartime witches, ghosts and smugglers abound in this dual-time supernatural mystery story. In the summer of 1940, twelve-year olds Lawrence and Rachel are evacuated to the village of Burley in the New Forest. One night, they witness a group of people dressed in strange clothing creeping into the woods. Before long, they find themselves drawn into an adventure while the very future of their country is at stake.

In 1990, teenagers Nick and Molly uncover a diary in the attic which belonged to Molly's grandmother who was evacuated to Burley 50 years before. The diary hints at extraordinary events but creates more questions than answers before coming to an abrupt end. As they are drawn further into danger, can Nick and Molly find out what really happened in 1940?

Sim's Magic Windmill

Persimmon McStandish is twelve years old and has Crohn's Disease. But that's not her only problem. When she goes to stay with her Great Uncle Baldwin on the remote Isle of Eigg she stumbles across a magic windmill and finds herself drawn into an incredible adventure. Everyone seems to believe she is the heroine predicted in an ancient prophecy who must save Scotland from disaster, but Persimmon is not convinced.

Join her in a tale of friendship, heroism and redemption as she meets strange and magical creatures based on Scottish folklore and comes to terms not only with her destiny, but also with her illness.

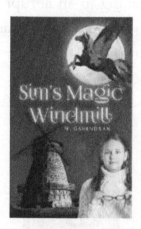

Saffron Moon

Life isn't easy for herbalists in 17th century London, but it's all Fen has ever known. When her Mam dies one harsh winter and she overhears a plot to assassinate a Lord, her life turns upside down forever. With only her herbs and a horse she embarks on the longest journey of her life to escape the conspirators who want to ensure her silence at all costs.

In 2015, everything seems to be falling apart for Leah Culpeper. Her Gran's Parkinson's Disease is worsening and to make matters worse, Leah loses her job and is left unsure of what to do with her life. When she finds an old manuscript in Gran's attic, she wonders what it has to do with her family history and whether the famous herbalist Nicholas Culpeper was one of her ancestors. As Leah finds the answers to these questions, she also begins to find herself.

Made in the USA
Monee, IL
02 January 2024

50962184R00121